Hare Krishna
Hare Krishna
Krishna Krishna
Hare Hare
Hare Rama
Hare Rama
Rama Rama
Hare Hare

Clever Fox Publishing
Chennai • Bangalore

MY JOURNEY OF LIFE

MY JOURNEY OF LIFE

A Narration On Battling CANCER
Through NATUROPATHY DIET

T.N. Jaggi

ISBN 13: 978-93-89604-32-0
ISBN 10: 93-89604-32-X

Published by CLEVER FOX PUBLISHING

List of Contents

Review by Renowned Doctor

Dr.HARSH DUA, M.D., Senior Consultant
Medical Oncology and Haematology
Indraprastha Apollo Hospital, Sarita Vihar,
New Delhi, 110044

This is to certify that Shri Trebhawan Nath Jaggi was my Non-Hodgkin Lymphoma Cancer patient from April 2010 to July 2011 as Indoor Patient and thereafter till date my Out Door Patient. He was given treatment of Chemotherapy for his NHL cancer which had advanced to B- IV stage and his attending Doctors in Mayo Clinic USA had estimated a life span of about 3 months only.

He has described the details of his treatment in his Biography Book. Very few patients like him are sincere and confident in following the Doctor's advice.

He also followed my advice on Diet to have a Balanced Nutrient Diet, during and after Chemotherapy treatment, to build his damaged/weakened Immune System by Chemo medicines.

Cancer Patients who have a strong will and determination and are prepared to follow their Doctor/Oncologist's advice, are sure to win their fight against Cancer Ailment.

Sd./
Dr. HARSH DUA

Review by Renowned Doctors

Dr. JAGPAL SINGH SAINI MD-MS, DMC
Regd.No. 49710
Senior General Physician&Surgeon
Awadh Health Care, SULTANPUR, DELHI

Shri Jaggi in his Biography Book "Cancer Ailment, Treatment and Naturopathy Supplementary Diet/Food Therapy" has given the details of his Cancer Ailment, 'Non-Hodgkin Lymphoma' and 'Prostate'. Since his NHL Cancer ailment had advanced to B-4 stage, he went for Chemotherapy for his NHL cancer ailment. Side by side with this treatment of chemotherapy he took the Supplementary treatment of Naturopathy and Diet/Food Therapy in consultation with his doctors, Oncologist and Naturopath. He continued his Supplementary Naturopathy treatment even after chemotherapy. This repaired his body's damaged Immune system to fight with cancer cells and thus he recovered back his heath.

I as Naturopathy Physician have reviewed Mr Jaggi's Biography of 'Cancer Ailment and Treatment and Naturopathy Supplementary Treatment.'. He has very ably given the gist of his study and Cancer Ailment, Treatment and Naturopathy Supplementary Food/Diet Treatment taken by him to recover from his Cancer Ailment.

Sd./
Dr. JAGPAL SINGH SAINI

Review by Naturopath Physiotherapist

Dr. SHAMBHU JAINWAL
B.Sc, M.A Yoga, Acupressure, Naturopathy, Punchgauv Therapy, Master Degree in Rekhi

Shri Jaggi in his Biography of his Cancer Treatment has described in detail the Naturopathy Physiotherapy treatment of

a) De-toxing the body
b) Practicing Yoga Exercises of Pranayama and body joints
c) Ayurveda Body Massage and Steam Bath
d) Acupressure
e) Taking Food/Diet required by the body to provide balanced Nutrition and
f) Avoid taking Foods which are against the natural system of the body and leave acidic residue in the body.

Shri Jaggi has followed the Naturopathy treatment under the able guidance of Naturopath Physiotherapist of Sevakram Naturopathy Centre, at Lajpat Bhawan, NewDelhi. I recommend that those needing the Naturopathic treatment of their ailment should follow the advice of Shri Jaggi and follow the Naturopathy treatment under the guidance of an able and experienced Naturopathy Doctor and Physiotherapist.

Sd./
Dr. SHAMBU JAINWAL

Author's Son: Sandeep Jaggi

Foreword

CANCER IS A killer in its truest form—it might be a nightmare for a few, but for some it becomes a reality, knocking right through our door, in the moment we least expect it; catching us off guard.

My father was a survivor. He was nothing short of that. He lived a complete life of 90 years, never having to eat a single medicine in his life till he was diagnosed with cancer. Being a renowned mining engineer, he held many senior positions in the Government of India and was awarded a gold medal from Mining Geological & Metallurgical Institute of India (MGMI). He was a very meticulous man—climbing both government and corporate ladders to the top of his field—serving as a chairman and leader to so many. He had his own persona, working till the age of 80 years, even after retirement as a senior consultant. The way he lived his life was admirable and he was an example not just to us, but to everyone around him.

He taught me strength, resilience, and persistence. His battle with cancer lasted eight long years, starting January 2010 and there was not a brief moment in which we saw him give up or not display a positive frame of mind. He accepted everything that was thrown at him with a smile, never letting either me or our family even get a glimpse of his pain or internal battle. He was a fighter.

This book was written by him with an intention to help fellow patients going through the big C. He wished to make a difference by providing his insight over the understanding of this disease, the changes it makes in the body, and the overall damage it does. He wrote this self-help book to raise the importance of positive thinking and having a positive attitude in life despite what is thrown at you. The importance of knowing your own body, which we often forget to take care of. The need to eat right, not diet. The need to exercise, to stay fit. Moreover, the need to question, understand, and accept. And lastly, embrace.

His main goal was to strike a personal chord with his readers by narrating his own life's story of battling cancer, his own personal experience, feelings, and steps taken to keep the mind as well as the body healthy. He has also written pages describing his line of treatment along with the names of doctors and hospitals he visited, both in India and abroad. This is written after great research and after reading a lot of books as food for thought.

Unfortunately, my father is not alive to publish this book, but being his son, I have taken it upon me to not let his writing and wish to go to waste. This is an ode to him—to the lovely father he was, a man of steel, and our backbone. I hope this is of some help to the readers and what is written is of some substance to add value to your life.

Thank you
Sandeep Jaggi
(son of T.N Jaggi)

Disclaimer

THE CONTENT OF this booklet is a Biography narration of author's Cancer Ailment, Treatment. This is provided for reference and educational purposes only. The content is not meant to be complete or to be applicable to any specific individual's medical condition. Therefore official sources of medical information should always be checked. A Reference List of Books and Literature, in this regard, has been given at the end of this booklet.

Further the information on Treatment provided should not be used to diagnose or treat a health problem or disease, nor overrule a diagnosis by a qualified health care provider. Do not use the information provided without consulting a qualified health care practitioner, Oncologist.

All the guide lines for food/diet indicated in this booklet are based on the personal experience of the writer which he obtained during his *Cancer treatment* and *Supplementary Food Therapy* from the top experienced Oncologists, Physicians and Naturopaths in India as well as abroad. All human bodies are not same. A particular food suiting one person may not suit another person. The recommended literature at the end of Booklet provides education and guidelines to patients including *Complementary Therapies*, and *Supplementary Therapies of Naturopathy & Diet.*

Preamble

CANCER AILMENT IS deadly terminal ailment and generally believed to bring death warrants to the patient. However this is not so. Death Warrants of Cancer ailment are cancellable and the ailment curable provided

(1) Patient follows Doctor's Advice both Pre, During, and Post Treatment stages of Cancer Treatment'
(2) Patient adopts a Positive Mind to get well.
(3) Patient has the Support of his near and dear ones to fight the ailment.
(4) Patient Co-operates with the attending Doctor to implement his treatment procedure including Nursing and Food/ Diet Plans which are equally important as administration of drugs for cancer treatment.

The writer gives below a brief history of T.N.Jaggi who suffered with cancer ailment and how he fought with his advanced D- IV stage Lymphoma Cancer. The diagnosing doctor of Mayo Clinic of USA, had estimated a maximum of 3 months time of cancer spreading to the other vital organs of the body which would then become irreversible and will lead to his death.

Author's Wife: Late Kamlesh Jaggi

Author's family

Acknowledgements

THE WRITER MR.TREBHAWAN Nath Jaggi would like to acknowledge the following.... *I THANK GOD EVERYDAY FOR EVERYDAY HE HAS GIVEN ME!!!!* My late wife Kamlesh Jaggi for being my mental & spiritual support from even higher up there. Her spiritual faith gave me the *courage and will power* to keep on going during my illness and gives me strength even today, to this day. It made me look at life with a lens of hope!

To my family for staying at my beck and call every day. I cannot stress this enough how much indebted I am to my children and grand-children for their love & support. Seeing their utmost love and affection, gave me the courage and motivation to fight this deadly disease and overcome every hurdle thrown at me.

I am also thankful to all the doctors and nurses who cared & shared their brilliant talents with me in India as well as abroad in USA.

To Dr.Patric B. Johnson, M.D.,Ph.D. Department of Internal Medicine/Division of Haematology, Blood and Marrow Transplant, Mayo Clinic, Rochester, Minnesota USA, who conducted all clinical investigation at Mayo Clinic and Diagnosed my B-IV Non-Hodgkin Lymphoma Cancer and asked his Secretary to give me and my family advice about Cancer ailment and treatment and how to face the Chemotherapy, which was the only treatment left for my survival.

To the team of intelligent doctors in Indrapastha Apollo Hospital headed by Dr. Jaideep Gupta, Dr. Harsh Dua, Senior Consultant, Haematology, Oncology, and Dr. Bimal Kapur, Senior Consultant Gastro logy, his team Dr. Kriplani Senior Surgeon Gastro logy.

To Dr. Vandana Nehra (*Gastroenterologist in Mayo Clinic, MN USA*) and Dr. Ajay Nehra (*senior professor of Urology in Mayo Clinic, MN USA*) for being perfect coaches and mentor throughout my illness. Words are just not enough to begin to express the gratitude and thanks for all the selfless help, support and guidance they showered upon me.

To the Naturopathic Centre at Lajpat Nagar, New Delhi, to all its workers, for their utmost hard work in taking such good care of me and giving me Naturopathic advice and treatment which gave me a second life this day and giving me ongoing care & support in helping me to achieve my goals.

I am indebted to the author of two Naturopathy Books, Mr.A.P. Dewan namely (a) Back To Nature For Healthy Living and (b) Food for Health. The information in these two books of Naturopathy along with advice given by Naturopathic Centre at Lajpat Nagar, New Delhi was fully utilised by me to regain my health after Emergency Operation of my Intestine in April 2011, to remove the infected potion of Intestine and join back of two portions if Intestine, one in the Colostomy Bag and the second the left over portion in the body during the Emergency Operation in April 2010 during Chemotherapy treatment.

JANUARY 2017

Chapter 1

Brief History of Writer's Cancer Ailment and Treatment

Personal note by the writer – Mr T.N. Jaggi (89yrs old):

THE INFORMATION PROVIDED and the statements made in this booklet are all my personal experiences that I learnt in my journey of life/rebirth. I was 82 yrs. old when I was first diagnosed with **Stage B-IV Non Hodgkin Lymphoma** with a **12x8 cm tumour** surrounding my intestine ready to burst anytime if not treated quickly. I was given only three months to live by the doctors. Doctors warned that if left it untreated, there will be no guarantee of recovery from the ailment later, due to advanced stage, B-IV and fast growing Cancer Ailment.

My wife had just passed away a few months back , I had not even recovered, out of this horrible shock, when this additional bombshell was dropped on me. My kids and grand kids were already extremely upset and heartbroken from losing their mom & grand mom respectively. This horrifying mind boggling news shattered them even further. I couldn't let that happen; I had to do something rise up to this tough development and make myself hale & hearty and available to them. I & my wife had some work still left as parents to do before we go for ever. Her unexpected death had no doubt left me alone to fulfil the left over tasks but I was ready to face this challenge God had thrown upon me. I decided I will fight this war against Cancer. It was not easy, lots of rocky & thorny bumps made it impossible at times to see myself get out of this scary, dark hole. It was a long journey but with the help of my family; their love and support and *An Angel* - my wife, who was supporting me even from up there, watching my every move I was able to get out of this ALIVE!

In order for you to fully appreciate the pre and post Guide Lines mentioned in this book I feel it is necessary to briefly describe my history of Cancer Ailment.

On February 2010, I went for a routine ultra sound exam for my chronic enlarged Be- nigh Prostate. Although the Prostate results came back with no significant changes, the ultra sound showed presence of a large tumour about 12x8 cm wrapped around my small intestine.

Further C.T. scan confirmed the tumour and presence of lymphatic lesion in other parts of my body and recommended *Big Needle Test* to rule out if the tumour and the lymphatic lesions present were cancerous.

The Big needle test came with its own set of problems. There was a chance that while performing this kind of test, the tumour could burst; causing further complications. I was not confident of this particular kind of tests/investigation in Delhi and decided to get this test done abroad. I went to the world renowned hospital in USA, Mayo Clinic in Rochester MN where FNAC Biopsy along with other tests were done which confirmed that I had *Non-Hodgkin Lymphoma – B-IV stage Cancer.*

The Oncologist in Mayo Clinic laid out a detail treatment plan and recommended 6 cycles of Chemotherapy for 80 - 90% cure of the disease. They advised an immediate treatment, as Cancer was fast growing (Tumour size had increased from 8 cm to 12 cm in one month) and would not take more than three months to spread to other vital organs of the body. Thereafter treatment/cure will be impossible and it will lead to Death.

Mayo Clinic confirmed that the Chemotherapy treatment suggested by them can be taken in India, but the treatment must be started either in India or In Mayo Clinic immediately. Luckily we found a well renowned Senior Consultant Oncologist/Haematologist – Dr Harsh Dua in Delhi Apollo Hospital. He confirmed over phone to my doctor in USA, that suggested Chemotherapy treatment can be given in Apollo. He also confirmed that Chemo medicines imported from USA are also available in Delhi.

I decided to leave for India with my daughter immediately and I visited Dr. Harsh Dua on 31st March-2010 in Apollo Hospital to discuss my Ailment and the line of treatment.

The first round of chemotherapy was started on 2nd April-2010, after taking a PET SCAN of my body. Three days into the treatment I developed a huge distension in my stomach with unbearable pain and high fever. I was quickly taken to the Emergency at Delhi Apollo Hospital. Further tests showed a rupture in the tumour. An emergency surgery was performed right away in which the affected intestine was cut, 6ft. of healthy intestine from the stomach was isolated and end taken out from the abdomen by making a hole in the abdomen. A Colostomy bag was attached to this 6 ft. portion of the Intestine for the discharge of excreta. The balance intestine was just left in the abdomen to be taken care after the treatment.

The treatment continued with balance five rounds of chemo sessions, each after every 21 days with a lot of challenge and stress to my body. However various tests, including Pet Scan, showed that body was now clear of Cancer. Barium Meal and other tests showed that even the left over portion of Cancer infected Intestine was clear of Cancer and was showing normal movement.

The 6ft of intestine left after the surgery to assimilate the nutrients from the diet was not enough for my body to function properly. Six months into the series of chemo treatment with no proper diet to the body, I was reduced from 75kg to mere 50 kg in body weight.

My treating Doctors at Apollo opined that now that the affected Intestine left over in the Body was clear of Cancer we can think of joining back two portions Intestine but the Doctors were not confident that my weak body will be able to undergo and sustain another operation.

For me the worst was still not over since I had very little intestine to deal with assimilation of any kind of nutrients into my body. It was a challenge for me and my family to keep me well nourished & healthy. I sent copies of my reports to expert doctors in Mayo Clinic in USA and Berlin thro' my brother. They agreed with assessment of Apollo Doctors. Telephone consultation/discussion between them suggested to try feeding of PTN nutrient thro' I.V. for a week, and test the body for improvement in body nutrient uptake and if positive, go ahead with operation and join back the healthy portions of the two parts of the intestine.

Feeding of PTN nutrient did not give confidence and positive signal to my treating Doctors. Lots of different ways and means were adopted/ tried out to deal with this difficult situation but my weight would not budge. It was getting hard for me to gain any weight.

In April' of 2011 fortunately or unfortunately I developed a fatal infection in my 6 ft. intestine attached with the colostomy bag. As a result I had to be operated in an emergency and the doctors were able to discard the infected intestine and re-join the rest of them together. Now I was back to being normal as far as my bodily functions were concerned but the body left was just skin & bones with weight of 44kg and no bodily strength what so ever....

All of this trauma had made my body very weak and fragile. After trying practically everything for recouping and regaining back my strength and not succeeding I decided to try Naturopathy. My family and I had tried everything else but it was always like taking one step forward to two steps backwards the next day. To my luck Naturopathy way of self-healing was just what my body needed, I started following it to the T. It took time but I started to show improvement day by day. From a body weight of mere 44kg in the year 2011 to body weight of 70kg by the end of year 2014 and now normal weight of 75 kg. in Dec. 2015 and normal blood chemistry. I give below my photographs.

a) in March 2010, before starting of Chemotherapy treatment
b) in April 2011, before joining back of two portions of Intestine
c) in December 2014, after recouping.

(a) (b) (c)

I'm a firm believer and a great living example to this remarkable way of life. Natural Food Articles and Herbs are the **nuggets of nature** which we as humans have just ignored. I strongly urge everyone to follow this as much as they can even if not 100%. Naturopathic Style of Living and Diet, will be an investment towards your *BANK OF HEALTH!* Good luck to all & May god bless you with Good Health, Wealth & Happiness

CHAPTER 2

Overview of Cancer Ailment and Treatment

LYMPHOMA CANCER RESEARCH Foundation, USA has made the following **'Over Review of Cancer'**

What is Cancer?

Cancer is the general name for a group of more than 100 diseases. Although there are many kinds of cancer, all cancers start, because abnormal cells grow out of control. Untreated cancers can cause serious illness and death.

Our bodies consist of millions of cells that grow and divide in an orderly fashion and work in harmony to support thousands of biological functions. The good cells divide only when it is necessary to replace the worn- out or dying cells.

Cancer is a group of diseases that as a result of the uncontrolled growth and spread of abnormal cells. Cancer cells are different from normal cells because instead of dying in an orderly fashion, they continue to grow and divide, forming new abnormal cells.

Cancer cells develop when there is a damage to the DNA, the hereditary material found in every cell, that is caused either by inherited DNA cell abnormalities and/or exposure to something in the environments, such as a),exposure to micro dust b)smoking, c) exposure to chemicals such as pesticides,fertilizers,0rganic solvents, HIV/AIDS,

Hepatitis. Usually the body is able to destroy these damaged cells, but when the body's natural defence systems do not work sufficiently, these abnormal cells may grow in an uncontrollable fashion, eventually forming a "Cancerous Tumour."

No one knows the exact cause of most of the Cancers. We know that certain changes in our cells can cause cancer to start, but we don't yet know exactly how it all happens. Scientists are studying this problem and learning more about the many steps it takes to form Cancers.

Immune System of our body is the major defence system of our body against disease. The cells of Immune System work together to get rid of foreign invaders, such as bacteria, and viruses before they can harm the body. These invaders are detected by the proteins of the Immune system cells called the 'Antigens'. These Antigens together with the cells of the Immune system start acting to destroy the foreign invaders and remove them from the system.

How is cancer is diagnosed?

If your doctor suspects cancer you are likely to need more tests, such as x-rays, blood tests, or a biopsy. In most cases a biopsy is the only way to be sure whether or not cancer is present.

To do a biopsy a piece of the lump of abnormal area is taken out and sent to the laboratory. There a pathologist (a doctor who specializes in diagnosing diseases) looks at the cells under a microscope to see if cancer cells are present. If there are cancer cells, the doctor tries to figure out what type of cancer it is and whether it is likely to grow slowly or more quickly.

Scans can measure the size of the cancer and can often show if it has spread to nearby tissues. Blood tests can tell doctors about one's overall health, show how well your organs are working, and give information about blood chemistry.

How is cancer treated?

The most common cancer treatments is Surgery, Radiation Therapy, and Chemotherapy. These therapies may be used either alone or in combination with other Therapies. Other Cancer treatment options include targeted Therapy, immunotherapy, hormonal therapy, and stem cell/ bone marrow transplantation.

Alternate Therapies are Homeopathy and Ayurveda. These treatments have been successful in a few cases.

Naturopathy Therapy is mostly used as Supplementary Therapy only. In rare cases of early stage of Cancer, it has worked as main Therapy of Cancer

Before beginning a Cancer treatment, consider asking the doctor about the goals of treatment, how long the treatment will take, and the potential side effects. Knowing what to expect before treatment begins, helps to reduce any fear and anxiety you may be feeling about your cancer treatment plan. It is also important that people with cancer and their families feel comfortable about their doctor and his or her recommended treatment plan. It is always appropriate to seek a second opinion to build the confidence of the patient in the treatment.

Going to the Doctor/Oncologist

Your relationship with your doctor is a key part of your care. Your doctor will explain your diagnosis, your health condition, your treatment options, and your progress throughout treatment.

Questions the Patient or his family should ask:

- What type of cancer? What is the stage or extent of the cancer?
- What is the outlook for the future (prognosis), as you see it?
- What treatment do you suggest and why?
- What is the goal of treatment – to cure or to control symptoms?

- What are the possible risks or side effects of treatment?
- How long will treatment last?
- What are the names of the drugs? What are they for?
- What other drugs or treatments options are there?
- How will we know whether the treatment is working?
- What symptoms or problems should I report right away?
- What are the chances that the cancer may come back (recur) with the treatment plans we have discussed?
- What can we do to be ready for treatment?
- Are there any special foods the patient should or should not eat?

Make sure that all your concerns and questions, no matter how small, have been answered.

Interpretation of the situation

Finding out, you have cancer, can present many changes for you and your loved ones. Simply having answers to your questions can help, you feel more in control and less worried about what lies ahead. The first question that comes up to many people's mind who have been told they have cancer is, "What did I do wrong?" or "Why me?" Because doctors don't know for sure what causes cancer in each case, many people come up with their own ideas about why they have the disease.

Some people believe they are being punished for something they did or failed to do in the past. Most people wonder if they did something to cause the cancer. Some think that if they had done something differently, they could have prevented the disease.

If you are having these feelings, it's important to know that you're not alone. All of these thoughts and beliefs are common among cancer patients. But cancer is not a punishment for things you did or didn't do in the past. Don't blame yourself or look for ways you might somehow have prevented cancer. Cancer is not your fault, and it's almost never possible to find out its exact cause. Focus instead on taking good care of yourself now, both physically and emotionally.

What can I do to take care of myself during chemo?

During your chemo, take special care of yourself. Your doctor or nurse will give you tips on how to do that. But there are some basic things you should do, such as:

a) **Get plenty of rest.** You may feel more tired than normal during treatment. Give yourself time for rest breaks when you need them.
b) **Eat healthy foods.** It's important for your body to get enough protein and calories to rebuild the healthy cells that it loses during treatment. Your doctor, nurse, or dietician may work with you to make sure you are eating the right foods to get what you need. If you have trouble eating or don't feel like eating, talk to your doctor or nurse.
c) **Get exercise and fresh air if your doctor says you can.** Exercise can help reduce stress and tiredness, and can help you feel like eating. Check with your doctor about your Exercise and Diet Plan to make sure it's OK.
d) **Check with your doctor or nurse before taking Vitamins or Supplements.** If you are already taking vitamins or supplements, tell your doctor what you take and ask if it's OK to keep taking them.
e) **Keep thinking about the treatment goals.** Dealing with chemo can be hard. A good way to handle the effects of chemo is to remind yourself why you're getting it. **Learn more about your cancer and treatment.** The more you know, the better you will be able to cope.

f) **Take time to enjoy your hobbies.** Doing the things you like to do can help you cope with chemo, too.

Precautions to prevent infections while on chemotherapy?

You are usually more prone to infections while you are having chemotherapy.

- Eat cooked food.
- Raw fruits and vegetables should be thoroughly washed.
- Drink boiled or mineral or R.O treated water.
- Wash your hands thoroughly, especially before eating.
- Use a soft toothbrush and take care of your mouth.
- Do not keep your nails long and cut them carefully.
- Ask your friends and family to wash their hands when coming into contact with you
- Avoid people with colds or the flu
- Avoid large crowds, which may include sick people
- Avoid crowded places where chances of contracting infection are more. You can wear a mask if you wish, but it is not mandatory.
- Use lotions rather than a razor to remove hair.
- Take a gentle bath and lightly dry the skin with a towel. Do not rub.
- Do not 'fiddle' with pimples and boils.

General Guidelines for when to Call Your Doctor

- Any side effect that lasts more than 1 day
- A fever of 100.5°F or higher, taken by mouth
- Bleeding
- Pain or redness at the IV site where the chemo was given
- Chills

- Cough or sore throat
- Severe constipation or loose stools or diarrhea over 24 hours
- Painful or frequent urination, or inability to urinate for more than 4 hours
- Mouth ulcers or sores in the throat or around the rectum.
- Unusual genital discharge or itching Redness, swelling, or soreness of the skin around an implanted port.
- **Safety Guidelines to be followed during Chemotherapy:**
- Flush toilets twice each time they are used. If possible, patients should use a separate toilet from others in the home. Always wash hands with soap and water after using the toilet.
- Care givers must wear gloves when handling the patients' blood, urine, stool, or emesis. Dispose of the gloves after each use and wash your hands.
- After using any devices for bodily waste, patients should thoroughly wash their hands and the devices with soap and water. Dry the devices with towels, and discard the towels.
- Any sheets or clothes soiled with bodily fluids should be machine-washed twice in hot water with regular laundry detergent. Do not hand wash. If you cannot wash them right away, place them in a sealed plastic bag.
- Absorbable undergarments should be place in sealed plastic bags for disposal.
- If care givers accidentally come in contact with bodily fluids, they should wash the area of exposure several times with soapy water and inform their doctors on their next visit. A single exposure may not do much harm, but caregivers should take extra precautions to avoid repeated exposure.
    - Be sure that someone is with the patient, because more help may be needed at those times.

Taking Care of Your Diet:

Chemotherapy, radiation, and other cancer treatments can be hard on the body. Fortunately, healthy food choices can help, feel better and speed the recovery. Ask your oncologist or a nutritionist if you need extra calories, vitamins and protein to keep up your strength during treatment.

Lack of appetite is common during cancer treatment. Some treatments can even make food taste unpleasant. Even though you don't feel like eating, it's important to get adequate nutrition.

- Choose high-calorie, nutrient-rich foods.
- Eat small meals throughout your day.
- Don't wait until you're hungry.
- Instead, eat at certain times of day.
- Keep your favourite foods close at hand. Certain foods can help ease the common discomforts from cancer treatment.
- **Monitor closely Ph of your body, salvia and urine. It should be maintained close to 7.3. This will create environments for strengthening of Immune System and death-knell conditions for Cancer Cells**
- **Conquer constipation** by drinking water and eating high- fibre foods like beans, lentils, vegetables, and fresh or dried fruit.
- **Drive away diarrhoea** with bland foods such as rice, bananas, and apples. Drink water to stay hydrated.
- **Protect mouth sores and avoid dry mouth** by grinding or pureeing foods to make them easier to swallow. Or eat foods that are already soft and mostly liquid, like soups and milk or yogurt shakes.
- **Nix nausea** by choosing bland foods and foods without strong odours. Steer clear of greasy foods. Go easy on your stomach

by eating small meals throughout the day. Drink plenty of water even if you are vomiting.

Cancer treatments temporarily weaken the immune system. So it's important to avoid germs that you can pick up from food. Contaminated food can make you quite sick. Here are some guidelines to help keep you safe.

- Avoid cracked or unrefrigerated eggs.
- Check expiration dates to avoid food spoilage, and throw away any mouldy foods.
- Cook all your meats until they're well done.
- Don't buy bulk foods from open bins, like salad greens.
- Keep all perishable foods in the fridge until you're ready to prepare them.
- Prepare your food on surfaces that are cleaned with soapy, hot water.
- Use a separate cutting board for raw meat, fish, or poultry. Wash it thoroughly after each use.
- Scrub and rinse fruits and vegetables thoroughly in Potassium Per magnate water
- Don't eat any fruits or vegetables that you can't wash easily, such as raspberries. Scrub the outsides, even if you don't eat them, like the rind of a melon.

The basic philosophy of Food/Diet for treatment of cancer is to strengthen the good cells/ Immune system. This is best achieved by taking good diet and drinks and avoid those which weaken the Immune system. The foods you choose to eat during active cancer treatment will vary according to any side effects you may be experiencing.

Overall, try to make food choices that provide you enough calories-to maintain your weight, protein-to help rebuild tissues that cancer treatment may have harmed the nutrients such as vitamins and minerals, and fluids- essential for your body's functioning.

Chapter 3

Moniteering of Cancer Treatment

1. The writer regularly monitored his body system, after completion of Chemotherapy treatment in Oct.2010, by Pet Scan, every 6 months for first three years and thereafter once every year. All Pet Scan pictures were free of Cancer till Jan. 2016.
2. The writer also monitored regularly his Blood Picture every three months for CBC(Complete Blood Chemistry), KFT(Kidney function test), LFT(Liver function test), Thyroid, Magnesium, Calcium, Iron, Vitamin D, B-12, Lipid profile, Diabetic Screening and Thyroid test.
3. Blood tests showed various values at different times. Writer altered his diet to make up the deficiency, taking the help of his Doctors, Oncologists & Natrupaths and Naturopathy books, namely. a) " Food For Health" by A.P. Dewan, published by Naturopathy Centre, Lajpat Bhawan, New Delhi. And b). " Healthy Living, Back to Nature" by A.P. Dewan, published by Naturopathy Centre, Lajpat Bhawan, New Delhi.
4. The writer also monitored his lower Abdomen, Kidney, Bladder, Prostate by Ultra Sound every year which were unremarkable. did Writer did not monitor its PSA level as he had Benign Prostate Enlargement.
5. **Pet Scan test done on 30 Jan. 2016, showed the presence of a Shadow in the 1.3 Vertebra Bone.**

6. Further investigation showed high value of PSA, 20.3 ng/ml
7. Subsequently Biopsy of Prostate gland showed 70% tissue affected by Cancer, confirming the revival of Cancer cells and spreading to other body cells

Chapter 4

Prostate Cancer Treatment

WRITER CONSULTED HIS doctor Dr. Harsh Dua, Senior Consultant Apollo Hospital, New Delhi for his Prostate Cancer. He ruled out Chemotherapy or Radiation Therapy for treatment of his Prostate Cancer, as his age was past 70 years. Instead the Doctor chose and started Medical Therapy) for treatment of his Carcinoma Prostate Metastatic from April 2016.

. Side by side the writer utilised his Naturopathy Advice/ knowledge and maintained his body ph. between 7.3 and 8.0 by increasing the intake of Alkaline foods and drinks, and stopping the Acidic foods and drinks. The body ph was monitored by checking the ph of saliva and urine in the morning with ph paper. In the first two months the writer maintained the body ph close to 8.0. **This reduced the PSA from 20.3 ng/ml, on 06 Feb 2016 to 8.24 ng/ml. on 03 March 2016 and 0.02 ng/ml in Nov.2016.**

The Pet Scan picture taken on 23 Feb. 2017 showed the absence of shadow or cancer in the L3 .L4 Vertebra Bone.

Chapter 5

Naturopathy

WHAT IS NATUROPATHY?

A system of alternative medicine based on the theory that diseases can be successfully treated or prevented without the use of drugs, by techniques such as control of diet, exercise, and massage, in short by 'Nature Care'.

Naturopathic medicine (called "naturopathy") is a distinct system of health care that emphasizes prevention and self-healing process through the use of natural therapies.

Naturopathic Doctors blend centuries-old knowledge and a philosophy that nature is the most effective healer, to build the damaged Immune System and stimulates the body's natural inherent power of healing itself with the help of five natural elements Jal (water), Vayu (air), Agni (fire), Akash (sky) and Prithvi (earth).

Thus Body has natural tendency to heal itself and Naturopathy only facilitates the process of healing through energy of nature.

KEY PRINCIPLES OF NATUROPATHY

1. **NATUROPATHY PLAN**

   Naturopathy is a way of life and methods that are followed in naturopathy which bring the person close to the elements of nature. It strives to bounce different elements of human body on a physical and spiritual level to attain good health.

Naturopathy, also called the "Nature Care" prescribes 'Return to Nature' for all physical ills. Basic principal working behind this Therapy is that ailments of the body are physical manifestation of weakness of body's organ. **The body's strong Defence Immune System is 'self curative' which comes into play to cure itself provided body's natural conditions, natural environments and proper food are followed.** Thus Naturopathy stimulates the body's natural inherent power of healing itself with the help of 5 natural elements like earth, air, fire, ether and water.

2. **Naturopathy Treatment consists of**
   2.1 Firstly diagnosing the Ailment,
   2.2 Secondly de-oxidising the patient by
   (a) cleaning the Colon by Enema, and Fasting
   (b) Body Massage, to clean and stimulate skin pores
   (c) Deep Breathing, to clean the Lungs and other vital organs by air (d) Steam Bath and
   (e) Regular practice of Jal Neti to clean the sinuses.
   2.3 Thirdly by proper Food/ Diet Management Plan, containing proper balance of quantities of Proteins, Carbohydrates, Vitamins, Minerals, Enzymes and
   2.4 Fourthly avoiding foods and drinks which upset the natural body balance and natural ph of body at about 7.3.
   2.5 Fifthly Acupressure or application of pressure at selected sites for specific disorders.

3. **Light Yoga Exercises.**
   (i) Breathing exercises to open the Lungs
   (ii) Light bending exercises to give movement to various body joints.

4. Holistic approach to Naturopathy

- Follow a healthy sleep pattern.
- Do not smoke.
- Avoid alcohol consumption.
- Do not eat if you are not hungry.
- Chew your food well.
- Eat fresh seasonal fruits & vegetables and not from cold storage.
- Follow a vegetarian diet.
- Avoid all kinds of processed, fried, sugary and spicy foods.
- Get up from the dining table with 50% full stomach. Remember all diseases begin in the Gut with over eating.
- Keep a cool mind while eating.
- Avoid all kinds of discussions while eating.
- Enjoy every bite to the fullest.
- Monitor the body's Elimination system e.g. stool & urine.
- Your perspiration and exhaling functions, to ensure removal of toxins from the body.
- Monitor the body's circulatory, respiratory and blood chemistry.

5. A Naturopathic diet

Eminent Doctors and Physicians have stated that Plants and Foods have a medicinal value and provide the required nutrients required by body organs for sustaining life. They are known to provide thoracic treatment to various ailments without causing any side effects. Here also, there are many living examples of Patients suffering from Diabetes, Cancer, High Blood Pressure, High Cholesterol, who have benefited with proper Yoga and Food/Diet Management Plan. Further if this Naturopathy

Yoga and Food/ Diet Management Plan is augmented, the *body's Immune System can be revived and it is possible to cure majority of chronic diseases, even Cancer by reviving* the Immune System.

Father of modern medicine, Dr. Hippocrates has stated "Our body has an amazing ability to heal itself, just give it the right environments and tools and it will do all the work for you." He has recommended, *"Let Food be your Medicine."*

- **<u>The healing power of nature</u>: The body has an inherent ability to maintain and restore health. Naturopathic physicians facilitate this healing process by removing obstacles to cure and identifying treatments to enhance healing.**
- **<u>Identify and treat the cause</u>: Naturopathic physicians treat the underlying causes of illness rather than just the symptoms of disease. Symptoms are an external manifestation of an internal imbalance due to any combination of physical, mental, or emotional causes.**
- **Symptom management may be important, but it is more important not to disregard the underlying cause of disease.**
- **A naturopathic treatment plan uses therapies that are gentle, non-invasive, effective, and do not have adverse side effects. A conscious effort is made to use methods that do not suppress symptoms.**
- **The primary role of naturopathic physicians is educating, empowering, and motivating patients to assume more personal responsibility for their health by adopting a healthy attitude, lifestyle, and diet.**
- **<u>Treat the whole person</u>: Naturopathic physicians identify specific weaknesses or dysfunctions in their patients and tailor treatment based upon the patient's individual**

presentation. It is the patient that is in need of treatment, not the disease state or symptom. Naturopathic physicians are interested in finding and treating characteristic symptoms that define the patient rather than common symptoms that define the disease.

Naturopaths have professed and shown that the

- Disease can be prevented/cured by following a proper dietary programme and natural living style. By making smart food choices, you can protect your health, feel better, and boost your ability to fight off cancer and other diseases by
- Drinking **fresh Juice from fruits & vegetables** prescribed to you
- Taking **balanced** quantities of Proteins, Carbohydrates, Vitamins, Minerals and enzymes from **natural food sources.**
- **Taking Herbal and botanical preparations,** including herbal extracts and teas. and

  Avoiding foods and drinks which upset the **natural body balance.** A poor diet stops the body from functioning well and builds-up toxins which can lead to wide range of illnesses.

CHAPTER 6

Naturopathy Plan for Cancer Treatment

EMINENT DOCTORS AND Physicians have stated that Plants and Foods have a medicinal value and provide the required nutrients required by body organs for sustaining life. They are known to provide thoracic treatment to various ailments without causing any side effects. Here also, there are many living examples of Patients suffering from Diabetes, Cancer, High Blood Pressure, High Cholesterol, Arthritis who have benefited with proper Yoga and Food/Diet Management Plan.

Further if this Naturopathy, Yoga and Food/ Diet Management Plan is augmented, the body's Immune System can be revived and it is possible to cure majority of chronic diseases, even Cancer.

According to a well-known Naturopath/Homeopath

Dr.Victor G Rocine....
"If you eat wrongly *No doctor can cure us;*
If you eat rightly *No doctor is needed;"*

Basic philosophy of Naturopathy Cancer Treatment is to strengthen the good cells and the Immune System._Naturopaths have professed and shown that this Cancer disease can be prevented / cured by following a proper Dietary Programme by which you remove deficiency of essential Nutrients, Minerals, Vitamins from the body through Food items which are readily absorbed and assimilated by the body.

Thus the Death Warrant/ Sentence of Cancer Ailment can be and have been cancelled with the above suggested Naturopathy Plan and Food Nutrition.

As stated above, Cancer Ailment manifests itself when our body's Immune System gets deranged apart from various reasons like Heredity, exposure to micro dust, acid, pesticide and fertiliser chemical fumes.

A Diet deficient in Nutrients plays a major role in the development of Cancer Ailment as deficiency of Nutrients weakens the Immune System of the body and good cells are not able to kill the Cancer Cells and throw them out of the body system.

Food/ Diet 0f Cancer patients both during and after Radiation or Chemotherapy treatment should be rich in above stated nutrients Protein, Calcium, Magnesium, Phosphorus, Potassium, Vitamins A, B, C, D, E and micro nutrients like Zinc, Selenium, Copper, Iodine etc. and dietary soluble and insoluble Fibres, Amino Acids, Anti Oxidants, so that body's immune system/cells get the required nourishment.

At the same time patient should avoid the foods which are the food of Cancer Cells for their growth. These Foods are

- Red Meat
- All forms of fried and spicy food items.
- Carbonated drinks like Coke & Pepsi

- **Refined flour in any form**
- **Polished rice.**
- **White sugar & sugar substitutes**
- **Noodles, pizzas, burgers, all kinds of fast food**
- **Excess sodium/salt**
- **Alcohol**

  This is best achieved by taking good Food/Diet and practices as mentioned below and avoiding foods which weaken the Immune System.

  Writer followed the following Naturopathic Dietary Plan

- **Took Foods/Diet** balanced in Protein, Vitamins, Minerals, Amino Acids, Anti-oxidants foods with Digestive enzymes, Fibres, both soluble and insoluble and with proper/adequate amount of fats and carbohydrates so as to give to the body the required amount of nutrients and energy/calories
- Writer followed the Diet Chart, given in chapter 12 of this Biography.
- **Avoided foods** which are difficult to digest and cause acidic reaction or leave behind acidic residues in the body in which Cancer cells thrive and multiply.
- **Took foods balanced in Alkalinity and Acidity. By nature our bodies PH is alkaline.** Too much acidic foods in the diet causes the PH levels to change from Alkaline to Acid which results in the body getting sick & prone to diseases, and provide food to ailment and cancer cells.
- **Salt intake was reduced** as it increases the tendency in the body to retain water which affects the uptake of essential vitamins and minerals from the food.
- **Said no to White sugar or sugar coated sweets** as they add only empty calories and do not have any food value.

- **Water Intake was adequately maintained at** about 8-10 glasses of water per day, including one glass of Lassi(chaj), one glass of Whey water(Channa pani) + one glass of green Coconut water. This amount of water is necessary to wash out/remove the toxins from Kidneys which filter and remove the salts from the blood and maintain water balance in the body to Keep the body hydrated.
- **Took foods with adequate amount of Fibres** so that intestines can throw out the solid residues left over.
- **Took Enema with 1200 ml of lukewarm water, once a week, in which Neem Tree leaves have been boiled.**
- **Said no to Alcohol and Carbonated drinks** specially **Colas** which contain Phosphoric Acid, and are highly acidic in reaction.
- **Regularly did physical exercise,** which helped to remove toxins from the body by perspiration and supplied oxygen to body organs.
- Occasionally took **Steam Bath,** to remove toxins from the body.
- **Did Yoga exercises**
  - a). Breathing/Pranayama, Kapalbharti, Anulom Vilom exercises for at least 15-20 minutes every day. This helped to give more intake of oxygen, to the body Organs thus improving the function.(These Pranayama exercises are a must for patients suffering from Leukaemia, Lung and other Cancers.)
  - b). Light bending exercises to give movements to various body joints, like shoulders, neck, hand, feet, knees, waist, hip, back etc.
  - c). Light walk for about 1.0 km. everyday.

- **Took Body Massage with Herbal Oil.** This was to revive/ rejuvenate the muscles, cells and nerves of thigh, calf and feet etc. which got weaker from Chemotherapy, Cancer treatment.
- Undertook Physiotherapy - Acupressure, Acupuncture, Magneto Therapy to revive the vital body organs.
- **Kept a positive** mind during treatment/therapy.
- **Avoided further** exposure to micro dust particles, poisonous gases and chemicals.
- **De- stressed the Body organs by Meditation.** This was to improve the Nervous System of the body.
- **Had good cancer support at home. This is essential and crucial.**

  <u>This family support to the writer, Patient helped him to fight his deadly disease.</u>
- **Had good friends, with Strong and Positive Mind, Will Power.**

  As stated above, Cancer Ailment manifests itself when our body's Immune System gets deranged. Apart from various reasons like Heredity, and Diet deficient in Nutrients plays a major role in the development of Cancer Ailment as deficiency of Nutrients weakens the Immune System of the body and good cells are not able to kill the Cancer Cells and throw them out of the body system.

  Food/ Diet 0f Cancer patients during and after Radiation or Chemotherapy treatment should be rich in Protein, Calcium, Magnesium, Phosphorus, Potassium, Vitamins A, B, C, D, E and micro nutrients like Zinc, Selenium, Copper, Iodine etc. and dietary soluble and insoluble Fibres, Amino Acids, so that body's immune system cells get the required nourishment.

Nature's laws ensure survival of the fittest. Our survival and how well we live depends upon our taking charge of our own health. Give to your body the nutrients it needs, to heal and maintain health,

'Food is medicine, increase your body's oxygen levels, and its ability to utilize and transport oxygen. Eliminate as many sources of toxins and poisons as possible. Improve your digestion and your body's ability to eliminate toxins.

Naturopaths have professed and shown that this disease can be prevented / cured by following a proper Dietary Programme by which you remove deficiency of essential Nutrients of Minerals, Vitamins from the body through Food items which are readily absorbed and assimilated by the body than chemical medicine/ vitamin supplements.

Cancer Patients should take Foods to build the Immune System of the body, which are Calcium, Magnesium, Potassium, Protein, Iodine etc.

Calcium – A great organic source of Calcium is Sesame Seeds which assimilates very well by the body. A tea spoon of Sesame Seeds contains Calcium equivalent to one tablet of calcium. For best results soak them in water overnight and take them with Breakfast. Other sources of Calcium are Cheese, Yogurt, Milk, Soybeans, Soy Milk, Sardines, dark leafy greens like Spinach, Kale, Turnips, and collard greens.

Magnesium -rich food, helps in assimilating calcium and vitamin C in the body. Organic source is Whole grain cereals, pulses, nuts, green leafy vegetables, beans, fish, Beta- carotene, Dairy products, provide a good source of magnesium to the body. With chemotherapy/cancer treatment magnesium in the body gets depleted. So intake of magnesium rich foods is necessary.

Potassium- rich foods help strengthen the nerves. Organic source is fresh green coconut water, asparagus juice, walnuts (akhroth), moth beans, black gram dal, green gram, Peas, whole wheat, almonds, cashew nuts, all help to improve the nerve disorder.

Amongst the fruit and vegetables Apples with skin, radish, onion, cucumber, baked potato, and amaranth are all good and contain Minerals - iodine, sulphur, silicon, potassium, selenium.

All the above minerals help in providing defence against cancer, mental disorders.

Selenium rich foods are Broccoli, Asparagus, Celery, Cucumber, Garlic, Onions, Mushrooms, Radish, Whole grains, Brown Rice, Sea Food, Kidney Beans. They act as anti-oxidant and boost the Immune System. A deficiency of selenium in the body can promote formation of cancer cells. Over cooking destroys the selenium in the food

Protein rich foods are Chicken, Fish, Egg Whites, Whole Wheat products, Brown Rice, Soya Bean, Tofu, Green Beans, Cottage Cheese, Masoor Dal, Black Gram Dal, Green Moong Dal, Wheat Germ, Wheat Sprouts, Moong Dal Sprouts, raw Almonds, Cashew Nuts, Peanuts, Walnuts, Methi seeds are great source of protein rich foods.

Iodine rich foods maintains Iodine level in the body. It keeps the Thyroid Gland in proper health which is essential for a healthy Immune System of the body. Iodine is a component of almost every living plant and animal. No standard measurements of iodine in food exist because iodine concentrations vary across the world. In general, foods from the sea contain the most iodine, followed by animal foods, and then plant foods. Of all foods seaweed, like kelp, is the most reliable source of natural iodine, however egg, dairy products, can also be of good source of Iodine.

Take Food with Enzymes which are necessary for the digestion of food and their assimilation in the blood. These Enzymes are provided by nature in the fruits and vegetables we eat. Over cooking them in any form destroys these enzymes. Saliva in your mouth has those enzymes which helps in breaking down the food by the process of chewing. More we chew the food in the mouth the greater is their absorption in the body.

Vitamin D - "sunshine vitamin" because it's produced in your skin in response to sunlight. Vitamin D is a fat-soluble vitamin in a family of compounds that includes vitamins D1, D2, and D3. It can affect as many as 2,000 genes in the body. Regular exposure to sunlight allows our skin cells to use ultraviolet-B rays to synthesize vitamin D, which has several benefits. Eating vitamin D enriched foods into your diet like fish, cod liver oil, milk, and eggs. Fresh fruits and vegetables are also good sources of vitamin D. It helps the intestine to absorb nutrients, including calcium and phosphorus.

This ensures strong bones and a strong immune system.

- Regulates blood pressure, reduces stress and tension, relieves body aches and pains by reducing muscle spasms, reduces respiratory infections, helps in differentiation of the cells, aids in insulin secretion, helps fight depression, improves overall skin health by reducing wrinkles, makes skin soft, strong, and smooth, and improves cardiovascular strength by providing a protective lining for the blood vessels.

At the same time patient should avoid the foods which are the food of Cancer Cells for their growth.

BALANCED ACIDIC & ALKAINE FOODS

On PH Scale Nuetral PH is 7.0 Body Ph 7.3

Foods above Ph of 7.5,or below 6.5 should be avoided as body's natural system cannot absorb/assimilate the nutrients from it properly

The Writer has broadly Classified various the various Foods as below

Foods below the Ph of 6,

Drinks. Alchol, Collas, Black Tea,Areated Waters

Foods. Red Meat, Tinned Fish, Pig meat, Slami, Deep Freezed Meat and Vegetables.

Fruits Blue Berries, Prunes,

White Atta, Rice, Sugar, Ice Creams

Foods above the Ph. Of 7.5-8.0

Lemons, Apple Cider Vinegar, Spinach Leaves Juice, Carrot Juice, Olive Oil, Asparagus, Papayas, Garlic, Broccli, Water Melon, Green Coconut Water, Almonds,

CHAPTER 7

Key Food Elements/Nature's Nuggets

THE WRITER STUDIED the food/nutrient value of various food items (Nuggets of Nature).These food items contain Proteins, Vitamins, Minerals, Fibres (soluble & Insoluble), Amino Acids.

I recommend detail reading of Book reference No.5

"Food for Health"

1. **CARROTS.** These are rich in Beta Carotene...Good Alkali food with lot of potassium, calcium, phosphorus, sulphur, sodium. Carrots nourish the optic system. It purifies the blood when taken with Cow Milk or Juice.
2. **CABBAGE**...High in Alkaline chemicals which help in blocking the Cancer Cells. Rich in Sulphur, Iodine, Chlorine. Its juice has a cleaning effect on mucus membrane. This speeds up the metabolism of oestrogen and is effective in healing Colon Cancer
3. **WHEAT BRAN**....is good source of insoluble Fibre. Take about 2 table spoon full per day. Take this added in Curd or soup oe warm milk. It acts as laxative and removes toxins from the body and helps to prevent Cancer of Intestine.
4. **AMLA....** (Goose Berry) ....has lot of anti- Cancer propertied. Recommended dose for Vit.C is 300 gm. of raw AMLA, which gives 2000mg of Vit. C. This boosts the Immune and Nerve system and inhibits the Cancer Cells from spreading.

5. **GREEN LEAFY VEGETABLES** enriched with vitamin-E serve as great source of anti-oxidants. They help in absorption of vitamin A & C. Prevent blood clot formation and improve blood circulation in the body. Eggs are another good source.
6. **TOMATOES & PUMPKIN SEEDS** enriched with vitamin K serve as blood anti-clotting system. Improve the function of Liver and Prostate gland in men.
7. **ASPARAGUS** is considered Queen of all vegetables. There are several success stories of Cancer treatment endorsing the use of Asparagus in their diet. Full soluble fibre, K & B group of vitamins which help in improving blood circulation.
8. **TURNIPS** are part of cruciferous vegetables. They contain high levels of antioxidants and phytonutrients associated with reduced risk of cancer. Research shows that plant compounds like glucosinolates help the liver process toxins, fight the effects of carcinogens and may even inhibit the growth of tumours.
9. **SUPER VEGGIES Broccoli, Cauliflower, Brussels Sprouts, Kale, Cabbage all members of the cruciferous, or cabbage, family of vegetables. And they all contain phytochemicals, vitamins and minerals, and fibre that are important to your health. Various components in cruciferous vegetables have been linked to lower cancer risks. Some have shown the ability to stop the growth of cancer cells for tumours in the breast, uterine lining (endometrium), lung, colon, liver, and cervix, according to the American Institute for Cancer Research. And studies that track the diets of people over time have found that diets high in cruciferous vegetables are linked to lower rates of Prostate Cancer.**
10. **FIGS -** each serving of dried figs provides 253 milligrams of potassium and 6 micrograms of vitamin K, or 7 percent of the

DV, along with 60 milligrams of calcium and 25 milligrams of magnesium, or 6 percent of the DV for these nutrients. Potassium is necessary for proper heart, muscle and digestive function. Your body uses vitamin K for blood clotting, calcium for strong bones and teeth and magnesium for immune system, heart and nerve function. It's very useful if soaked overnight & taken early morning.

11. **DATES** commonly known as 'Khajoor' are packed with essential nutrients, vitamins and minerals. They are rich in dietary Fibre, antioxidants, simple sugar and immediate energy to the body.
12. **ALMONDS** are rich in manganese, riboflavin, and copper, all of which aid in energy production. Contain a high level of monounsaturated fat, the same heart-healthy fat as olive oil. Vitamin E, also found in almonds, is an antioxidant that is very effective in reducing the risk of heart disease. Almonds are also high in magnesium, which improves blood flow and the movement of oxygen and nutrients throughout the body. Best when taken after soaking them in water overnight.
13. **WALNUTS** improve cardiovascular function and have wonderful anti-inflammatory properties. Although high in fats and concentrated in calories, the fats in walnuts are healthy fats. And Wall Nuts are a great source of fibre and protein and are considered as 'NERVE TONIC'
14. **MUNIKA** Grapes that are dried in a certain manner become Monika. Most of the helpful qualities of grapes can be found in Monika. It also contains high amounts of iron and vitamins needed by the body. As a result it assists people with anomie through increasing haemoglobin in the blood. It is also helpful in treating other diseases of the blood that are caused by chronic fevers and inflammation. Munakkas should be washed

and then soaked in water overnight. They should be taken on empty stomach first thing in the morning.

15. **PAPAYA FRUIT** rich sources of antioxidant nutrients such as carotenes, vitamin C and flavonoids; the B vitamins, folate and pantothenic acid; and the minerals, potassium, copper, and magnesium; and fibre. Together, these nutrients promote the health of the cardiovascular system and **also provide protection against Colon Cancer. Papaya fruit leaves Juice possess medicinal qualities. It improves the Blood Chemistry, especially Platelets. It is a regular therapy for Dengue and other blood infections.**

16. **GUVAVA.** One of the most celebrated and important benefits of adding guava to your diet is its ability to inhibit the growth and metastasis of Cancerous Cells. There have been numerous studies done in recent years on guava's effects primarily on prostate cancer, breast cancer, and oral cancers. Guava leaf oil is extremely successful as an anti-proliferative substance, and has actually been shown to be more effective than some leading modern medicines in reducing cancerous growth.

17. **BANANA or PLANTAIN** rich in potassium, phosphorus, sulphur, calcium, magnesium, iron, copper and iodine. It also contains Vitamin A, B, C, and E. Ripe Banana helps in curing chronic intestinal indigestion problems. Unripe Bananas cooked as vegetable and subsequently dried banana flour are good for patients suffering from Diabetes. Well ripened or boiled Bananas are good for peptic, gastric and duodenal ulcers. **Banana works well in both situations; constipation and diarrhoea.**

18. **TULSI (BASIL)** has unique power of purifying blood and killing bacteria. **It cleanses the intestine of toxic matter and body of all ailments like digestive, circulatory, respiratory,**

excretory, urinary, and nervous system. The Tulsi plant has many medicinal properties. The leaves are a nerve tonic and also sharpen memory. They promote the removal of the catarrhal matter and phlegm from the bronchial tube. The leaves strengthen the stomach and induce copious perspiration. The seed of the plant are mucilaginous Juice of Tulsi leaves with honey or tea cures the common cold. It acts as antiseptic and antibiotic.

19. **ALOE VERA contains over 200 active components including vitamins, minerals, amino acids, enzymes, polysaccharide, and fatty acids- no wonder it's used for such a wide range of remedies.** Aloe Vera is a well-known adaptogen. An adaptogen is something that boosts the body's natural ability to adapt to external changes and resist illness. It alkalizes the body, helping to balance acidic dietary habits. It contains 12 substances, including B-sisterly, which can help to slow down or inhibit inflammation. This may be able to help painful joints due to stiffness and help improve joint flexibility.

20. **WHEAT GRASS juice contains 97 enzymes, vitamins, phytochemicals and minerals which help in treatment of Cancer.**
    a. Detoxifies the Liver
    b. Cleanses the Colon
    c. Leads to a tangible energy boost
    d. Boosts the Immune System
    e. Purifies blood as Chlorophyll has similar molecular structure to hemoglobin – a component of blood
    f. Experience less colds as your resistance to infection increases contains more protein per once than meat.

21. **LEMONS** a good source of vitamin C. **Provides alkalinity to the body which neutralises the acidity/acidic residues in**

the body. In Naturopathy treatment of Cancer it is essential to maintain alkaline environments in the body as cancer cells do not progress in alkaline environments. Daily dosage is 2 lemons a day.

22. **HONEY** raw organic honey is loaded with vitamins, minerals, and enzymes which protect the body from bacteria and boost the immune system. Cold and flu symptoms, such as coughs, sore throats, and congestion are also kept at bay when treated with honey. **Drinking warm water with lemon and honey on an empty stomach, first thing in the morning on a daily basis is one of the best ways to cleanse the liver, remove toxins, and flush fat from the body.** Ayurveda prescribes intake of two spoons of Honey every day.

23. **GARLIC can used by all to cure health problems like diabetes, hypertension, jaundice, rheumatism, malaria, arthritis, asthma, bronchitis, common cold.**
    a. It lowers the blood cholesterol, improves the HDL/LDL ratio
    b. Improves the blood circulation, prevents blood from clotting
    c. Reduces the body's production of fat.
    d. It removes the plaque deposit from the arteries thus helps in normalising the Blood Pressure.
    e. It has antiseptic, antibiotic and antifungal properties.
    f. Those suffering from Piles and Dysentery should use only with doctor's advice.
    g. Best and effective way of taking is to take two cloves of garlic crushed to make a paste and swallow in an empty stomach with a full glass of water; preferably first thing in the morning.

h. Researchers from all over the world have established the medicinal value of Garlic.

24. **GINGER (ADRAK, SONTH) Fresh or dried ginger reduces the gastric secretions in the stomach. It reduces the stomach disorders of indigestion.** It has warm effect and thus should be avoided by those suffering from Piles and Dysentery.
    a. Eat fresh ginger just before lunch/dinner to stoke a dull appetite and fire up the digestive juices.
    b. Ginger improves the absorption and assimilation of essential nutrients in the body.
    c. Ginger clears the 'microcirculatory channels' of the body, including the pesky sinuses that tend to flare up from time to time.
    d. Feeling airsick or nauseous? Chew on ginger, preferably tossed in a little honey.
    e. Gas—oops—guess what? Ginger helps to reduce flatence.
    f. Tummy moaning and groaning under cramps? Munch on ginger.
    g. Reeling under joint pain? Ginger, with its anti-inflammatory properties—can bring relief.
    h. Just had surgery? Chewing ginger post-operation can help overcome nausea.
    i. Stir up some ginger tea to get rid of throat and nose congestion

25. **FLAX SEEDS some call it one of the most powerful plant foods on the planet. It may help reduce the risk of heart disease, cancer, stroke, and diabetes. Although flaxseed contains all sorts of healthy components, it owes its primary healthy reputation to three of them:**

a. **Omega-3 essential fatty acids, "good" fats that have been shown to have heart-healthy effects. Each tablespoon of ground flaxseed contains about 1.8 grams of plant omega-**3s.
b. Lingams, which have both plant estrogen and antioxidant qualities. Flaxseed contains 75 to 800 times more lingams than other plant foods.
c. Fibre. Flaxseed contains both the soluble and insoluble types.

26. **TRIPHALA** is made from the fruits of three trees that grown in India and the Middle East (the Sanskrit term triphala means '"three fruits": tri = three, and phala = fruits). The fruits are dried, ground into powder, and blended in a precise manner developed by the ancient herbalists Triphala is a valuable part of panchakarma because it gently cleanses and detoxifies the body without irritating the colon. In addition, unlike other laxatives that deplete the body, triphala actually strengthens and nourishes the bones, nervous system, and reproductive organs
27. **CUMIN or JEERA.** Improves Digestion. Cures IBS, Piles. Specific medicine for Diabetes, Asthma, Bronchitis, supplies Iron to the body, prevents development of Anima. Good source of Anti-oxidant, removes Free Radicals from the body and fights to remove Infection from the body.
28. **WHOLE GRAIN** These are low in Fat but posses good quality healthy Fibre required for healthy movement of bowls to throw out the Toxins.
29. **FAT free Dairy Products** like Milk, Yogurt, cheese These provide calcium , protein, minerals and , Vitamin B.
30. **BERRIES.** Rich in Anti-oxidants, which lower the risk of Cancer and cardiovascular disease. Blue Berries are far better than Black Berries, Raspberries and Strawberries.
31. **BROCCOLI.** These along with other cruciferous vegetables like Cabbage, Cauliflower, Kale, Brussels have naturally

occurring phyto-chemicals which reduce the risk of Cancer. They have fibre and no fat or cholesterol or calories.

32. **GREEN TEA.** This has phyto-chemicals which reduce the risk of various diseases and also inhibit the enzyme required for some cancers growth.
33. **BEET ROOT.** This has good health value. It contains Sodium Potassium. Its juice along with carrot juice cleans liver and kidneys. It is a good liver tonic. I It builds up red corpuscles, tone up the blood, tonic for anaemia.
34. **COLOURED FRUITS AND VEGETABLES**
    The colors of fruits and vegetables are a small clue as to what vitamins and nutrients are included. By getting a variety of different colored fruits and vegetables, you are guaranteed, a diverse amount of essential vitamins and minerals.

The phrase "***eating a rainbow***" of fruits and vegetables is a simple way of remembering to get as much color variety in your diet as possible, so that you can maximize your intake of a broad range of nutrients.

Each different color fruit and vegetable contains unique health components that are essential to our health.

Fruits and vegetables are very important to our health because they are whole foods, created by nature, that are rich in a large amount of nutrients. Eating plenty of healthy vegetables and fruits can help prevent heart disease, strokes, diverticulitis, blood pressure, some types of cancers, and can guard against cataract and macular degeneration or vision loss.

There are unique phytochemicals, or plant chemicals, that vary from color to color. These various compounds all do different things to protect our health. When it comes to selecting produce, there's no one tint that rises above the rest. We need the full spectrum. Here's what each color brings to you….

Red fruits and vegetables -- Contain nutrients such as lycopene, elegiac acid, Quercetin, and Hesperidin, to name a few. These nutrients reduce the risk of prostate cancer, lower blood pressure, reduce tumour growth and LDL cholesterol levels, scavenge harmful free-radicals, and support join tissue in arthritis case

Orange and Yellow fruits and vegetables - Contain beta-carotene, zeaxanthin, flavonoids, lycopene, potassium, and vitamin C. These nutrients reduce age-related macular degeneration and the risk of prostate cancer, lower LDL cholesterol and blood pressure, promote collagen formation and healthy joints, fight harmful free radicals, encourage alkaline balance, and work with magnesium and calcium to build healthy bones.

Green vegetables and fruit - Green vegetables contain chlorophyll, fiber, lutein, zeaxanthin, calcium, folate, vitamin C, calcium, and Beta-carotene. The nutrients found in these vegetables reduce cancer risks, lower blood pressure and LDL cholesterol levels, normalize digestion time, support retinal health and vision, fight harmful free-radicals, and boost immune system activity.

Blue and Purple fruits and vegetables - Contain nutrients which include lutein, zeaxanthin, resveratrol, vitamin C, fiber, flavonoids, elegiac acid, and quercetin. Similar to the previous nutrients, these nutrients support retinal health, lower LDL cholesterol, boost immune system activity, support healthy digestion, improve calcium and other mineral absorption, fight inflammation, reduce tumour growth, act as an ant carcinogens in the digestive tract, and limit the activity of cancer cells.

White fruits and vegetables - Contain nutrients such as beta- glucans, EGCG, SDG, and lingams that provide powerful immune boosting activity. These nutrients also activate natural killer B and T cells, reduce the risk of colon, breast, and prostate cancers, and balance hormone levels, reducing the risk of hormone-related cancers.

Chapter 8

Diet Chart of the Writer

This is a very personal /diet chart. This provides Balanced Nutrition. The writer has adopted to keep himself healthy & fit after his cancer illness.

Those suffering from any kind of life style illnesses, like diabetes, high blood pressure, asthma, heart conditions etc. will have to avoid certain foods. Their physician can help them to design it specifically for them.

- **Early Morning** – Two glasses of warm water with juice of one fresh lemon plus 2tbsp. Aloe Vera juice, 5 fresh leaves of Neem and five fresh leaves of Tulsi, five almonds plus two Akhrots (Wall Nuts) soaked overnight in water.
- **Yoga Exercise (in the nearby park or roof top) –** A brisk morning walk of about 1.0 km for 20 min., followed by 30 min. of yogic Pranayama (breathing exercise) & light stretching exercises(giving movements to each body joint). Note: Yoga and Pranayama exercises should be taken under the guidance of a Yoga teacher.
- **Back home** – A glass of freshly squeezed mixed fruit/vegetable juice.
- **Breakfast** – A bowl of warm whole grain oatmeal cereal consisting of raw oats or barley or wheat germ or crushed carrot etc. in cow'smilk with additional add on;
- 1 tsp Flax, Sesame, Pumpkin seeds (soaked overnight),

- five Munakkas (dry Grapes), 2 Anjeers (dry Figs)all soaked in water overnight.
- 5 Almonds + 2 Akhrots(Wall Nuts), soaked overnight in water. (skin of soaked Almonds should be removed)
- Two boiled eggs (without yellow) or ¼ cup of fresh cottage cheese
- One glass of Yogurt, Lassi/whey water or lemon/herbal Green Tea with organic honey
- **Mid-day snack -** A bowl of fresh fruit + ½ glass of fresh mixed vegetable juice of Carrot, Cabbage, Beetroot, Wheat Grass, 2 green Almas, Spinach, Cabbage etc.
- **Lunch –** A cup of vegetable/chicken soup
    - Two chapattis of whole grain/multigrain flour or a bowl of boiled brown rice
    - A cup of fresh seasonal vegetables or chicken stew or fish curry.
    - Cup of curd
    - A bowl of mixed fresh green salad of cucumber, lettuce,tomatos.
- **Mid afternoon snack -** A bowl of fresh fruit + ¼ cup of raw mixed nuts (almonds, walnuts, roasted black gram, pistachios, khajoor(Dates) etc. with herbal green tea with 5 leaves of Tulsi(Basil) and honey.
- **Dinner** – Mostly identical to lunch.
    - A cup of vegetable/chicken soup
    - Two chapattis of whole grain/multigrain flour or a bowl of boiled brown unpolished rice
    - A cup of vegetable(fresh & seasonal vegetables) or chicken stew or fish curry.
- **Night time -** 2/3 hrs before sleeping

- o 1/2 tsp of Triphala powder with a glass of warm water. This is a natural bowel cleanser that detoxifies the digestive system on daily basis. Alternatively take Wheat Bran husks with two tea spoon of Castor Oil or Paraffin Oil in a cup of warm milk.

Referance Books/Litrature on Cancer, Food Therapy

1. Understanding Non-Hodgkin Lymphoma. Published by LYMPHOMA Research Foundation USA.
2. National Cancer Institute USA, Book "Chemotherapy and You"
3. National Cancer Institute USA Book "Eating Hints for Cancer Patients"
4. Nutrition Guide Lines for Patients, Indraprasta Apollo Hospitals, India.
5. Naturopathy Book "Food For Health" by A.P. Dewan, published by Naturopathy Centre, Lajpat Bhawan, near Moolchand Metro Station, New Delhi.
6. Naturopathy Book "Healthy Living, Back to Nature" by A.P.Dewan, published by Naturopathy Centre, Lajpat Bhawan, near Moolchand Metro station, New Delhi
7. A Complete Hand Book on NATURE CURE. www.health library.com
8. Published Literature by "National Institute of Nutrition "on Food Values, Hyderabad, and Telangana, India.
9. Food for Health Literature published by Google on the Internet.
10. Articles on Diet Therapy by Dr. Shiksha Sharma in Bunch Magazine of Hindustan Times, New Delhi, India.

11. Foods That Heals, by Dr Bernard Jensen, published by Health Harmony, New Delhi.
12. Mayo Clinic Book of Alternative Medicine.
13. Naturopathy, Treatment for Common Diseases By Dr. Sneh Chatterjee, Principal Indian Institute of Naturopathy, Yoga, Acupressure, New Delhi 110024

Notes

Notes

Notes